TEARS OF THE OLD MAGICIAN

TEARS OF THE OLD MAGICIAN

LEONARD NATHAN

We must read *as if.*
—George Steiner

ORCHISES
WASHINGTON
2003

Library of Congress Cataloging-in-Publication Data
Nathan, Leonard, 1924-
Tears of the old magician / Leonard Nathan.
p.   cm.
ISBN 0-914061-93-3 (alk. paper)
I. Title.

PS3564.A849 T43   2003
811'54—dc21

20020768409

ACKNOWLEDGMENTS

Grateful acknowledgement is made to the following magazines for reprinting the following poems (sometimes in quite different form).

"A Man and His Dog"	*English Journal*
"Message," "Pilgrim's Progress"	*Iowa Review*
"Daughters of Music," "Gouache," "Recessional"	*Manoa*
"My Kind"	*The New Yorker*
"Falling"	*Northeast Corridor*
"Return of the Alchemist" "The Plague,"	*Poet Lore*
"Party"	*Poetry International*
"Affairs" "Of Human Bondage," "Self Portrait"	*Salmagundi*
"Trick or Treat"	*Slant*
"Recess," "Woman Running Through Rain"	*Texas Observer*
"Quartet	*Vespers*
"The Traveler," "Offerings"	*West Branch*

ORCHISES PRESS
P. O. BOX 20602
ALEXANDRIA
VIRGINIA
22320-1602

G 6 E 4 C 2 A

for CAROL

TABLE OF CONTENTS

I. Home Bodies

II. In the World

III. Nevertheless

I
HOME BODIES

The world is full of partial
stories that run parallel to
one another, beginning
and ending at odd times.
                —William James

KINDS

Memory is a tiny room lit
by a wan lamp. The radio plays
soft static but no one minds.

Father yawns. Mother yawns too
but hides it behind a hand. I knew
already I was not their child.

My kind never yawned. Alert, we waited
for our time (and wait still).
I yawn, thinking about it.

THE GREAT DEPRESSION

Father, alone, killed himself with my popgun,
catsup spread on his shirt front, body
stretched on the kitchen floor.

Mother, setting the groceries down (there weren't
that many), showed him no pity, so he jumped up
grinning, too late to help.

Thereafter I saw him from far-off eyes—
bad imitation of a a bloody death,
but close enough for a child.

TRICK OR TREAT

When the orphan came to our door, it was Halloween.
We thought he wanted a sweet—chocolate
perhaps or a nourishing apple.

We thought because he was inscrutably blind
and spoke only in tragic Greek
it was our pity he wanted.

When he held out his hands, we saw through his torn gloves,
he was like a boy down the street but masked
to help us face our terror.

OF HUMAN BONDAGE

Only a little ways now, my dear. The son
in the father's dream curses the road,
climbs to his feet and limps ahead.

The son dreams the father arrives too late
in the ill-lit moth-eaten twilight
where the mother dreams with her eyes open.

Only a little ways now and the sleepers will wake
alone to find the house empty,
time ticking slowly backwards.

RECOGNITIONS

Too late, your father turns out
after all to be only your father—
you should have known.

How beautifully he danced well
into his sixties, made little jokes
about forgetting.

At the end, his eyes shut, he saw
the world for what it was—nothing
he could help.

A MAN AND HIS DOG

Every day about dusk
an old man and his dog
pass slowly under my window.

The man is sort of gray, the dog
sort of brown, or the man is sort
of brown, and the dog sort of gray.

Don't be sad. Look at it like this—
every day about dusk they pass.
Even in rain they pass.

PILGRIM'S PROGRESS

He has come so far, so near, but sleep
bewilders him and he forgets why
he is here and where he is.

He stands in the middle of some final room
as in a dark wood, waiting for memory
to catch up. It won't.

Dawn arrives instead, a granddaughter
who leads him by the merest love
back to the wrong world.

PARTY

Some stayed out in the garden hushed under stars,
others went in bearing the crystal music
of ice in tall glasses.

We stood awhile in the doorway, wanting, it seems,
to be in two places at once and being
in neither very much.

It was hard to believe there really was a Finland
or Cape of Good Hope or even our own house
somewhere in the dark.

THE MESSAGE

It was about time and much too late
or much too early for words, and it was yes
maybe but also mostly no.

The messenger galloped off, leaving behind
nothing but the message and a chamber
choking on its own silence.

It was also about fate, the way the prince
stared at his father while the women wept
on the bloody stairs, wept and sang.

FALLING

Wherever you choose to stand in this world,
that place, firm as it feels,
is a place for falling.

In my own house I fell. A dark thing,
forgotten, struck my ankle
and I fell.

Some falls are so slow, you don't know
you're falling till years later. And may be
falling still.

MOVING FATHER TO THE REST HOME

To father, bound for the rest home, it's all over,
even the shouting as he watches us
sort through and judge the leavings of his life:

faded photos, expired medicines,
pajamas held up by safety pins,
cheerful get-well cards from the long dead.

We sit on the floor and pronounce—not this, this
perhaps. A few we hold awhile longer
before we shrug and let them slowly drop.

THE OGRE'S MOTHER

The ogre left a trail of blood
as he hobbled home to weep
on his mother's knees.

There, there, she said. The story
gave her few words,
fewer feelings.

There, there, she said, wondering
if tea would help, wondering
what was tea.

DOMESTIC BLISS

Peace in the fish bowl—a face swims slowly up,
curious, long gold sleeves swaying
in the silence of still water.

Beauty unambitious as Ophelia
stares out, satisfied, sinking slowly
to the white sand of the bottom.

There, the tiny wreck of a pirate ship
is all that's left of evil. The rest is sleep,
wide-eyed, dreamless.

APPEARANCES

What looked like love dancing on the terrace
was loss of balance down the sheer face
of panic, hands snatching at air.

What looked like all the comforts of home was a bed,
a bottle of pills, a glass of dusty water,
a clump of damp tissue.

What looked like renunciation was a house,
vacant except for the footsteps of a son
seeing that nothing was left behind.

THE GURNEY

In the long corridor of beige
acoustical tiles where no one casts a shadow,
there were three of us—

you with your regret, me
with my guilt, and the other, eyes shut,
strapped to the gurney.

Pain, ahead, receded slowly
into a white silence never quite
to be reached.

THE FAMILY HOUR

If we unlock the door to this old dream,
inside we'll find, under the drift of dust,
a life of many small comforts.

No story here, only repetition,
only Smoke, the graymalkin, watching
our every sly or sorry move.

About now, the princess comes on home,
arm in a sling, one eye swollen shut,
smile bitterer than ever.

TRYST

I too would like the tale to end here
on the creaky thirty-third stair where we pause
to listen to a cry that's barely human.

Black cypress shutters the moonlight. Water
whispers below. We are children again
at hide and seek with Gothic night.

And here is the key we were told never to turn
in the lock of the door of the little room
we were told never to enter.

END OF THE LINE

In the old cemetery at the end of the line,
on the unkempt grave of a child long since buried,
a baby angel perches.

It wants eternally to fly, spreads
its chipped wings and scans space
with vacant white fanatic eyes.

Lovers kneel to leave violets there,
already drooping, and take away a silence
that lasts all the way home.

DINING IN

No Symposium tonight—
Socrates is seeing Beauty
(or Truth) elsewhere.

So we stay home and practice the word
Love. It doesn't come easy
to mouths made for biting.

Meanwhile, the meat gets cold.
What are we waiting for? Pass
the bread. Pass the Love.

WAITING FOR YOU

Waiting for you, I have come to believe
that far off is just that—
far off. All else, illusion.

So what we see as near can also be
far off and hurt to touch, even
in the best of dreams.

I know this isn't wisdom, only someone
barely keeping time till you arrive
with truth—any old truth.

II
IN THE WORLD

And, more than all, a strangeness in the mind,
A feeling that I was not for that hour,
Nor for that place.
                        —William Wordsworth

THINKING TOWARD A GRAND SYNTHESIS

Dandruff on the wide black sleeve
of the ancient Chinese scholar, dandruff
and a stain from lunch.

But in his head snow is falling
on bamboo, each stalk a thought
the wind perfects.

The cleaning lady, dusting, notes
it all and smiles but, out of pity,
says nothing.

RECESS

Think of it this way, children:
the world given only once
is beautiful.

Recess, the children flee,
playing at war, meaning it.
She winds her shawl tighter.

And weeps softly for all
the ugly worlds still to be born
and no one ever to love them.

MIDDEN

Smoke over the dump at Brownsville,
smoke and crows over the too
too solid waste.

Trucks, full, enter all day,
depart empty, leaving night
alone with its starry self.

This, as you may have guessed, is about
spirit but also about smoke,
mostly about smoke.

NARCISSUS

Reborn a nineteenth-century German pastor,
gazing out at valleys, hills and woods—
"O green distance, I love thee!"

He also loved the Alpenglow at dusk,
in which his sorrow, climbing ever higher,
found its radiant home.

But most of all he loved the sky, to him
heaven, a great mirror, in which he saw
not himself, but God.

WEATHER

Days like this, wind tearing through high,
horse-tail clouds, everything wants to be
itself—no symbols in this world.

Leaves falling are falling leaves, and you,
raking them up, are you, glad to be
the sole user of your life.

On such a day Prospero drowned his book
and departed, leaving a vast clarity
behind with nothing to fill it.

CONCENTRATION

Listen to the rain long enough
and it begins to make some sense,
not, of course, our kind.

Watching yellow leaves spin down a while,
we see a sort of pattern here,
not one of ours but close.

Being what we seem for whole hours,
we think we're only ourselves, not,
we admit, the ones we hoped.

WEB SITE

The storm that took the spider, left behind
only a tiny fan of moth wings
in its web, and a fallen leaf—

black and red, colors of disaster,
colors too of autumn sinking
into itself like fire.

The sky—I'd almost forgotten the sky—blue
whichever way I turn, color
of blessed emptiness.

DAY OF THE CONQUISTADORS

A day of glitter and yellow dust, of distance
curving hugely back on itself
in great gusts of light.

Our scouts, their eyes hollow, report a sea
of gold flowers and then, what
we only imagine:

A day of breastplates' advance, each reflecting
a whole kingdom just beyond
the next mirage. Or the next.

BREAKING CAMP

A huge bonfire fed
by the prisoners—ours, it seems.
Twilight full of smoke and shouts.

Their dog, Max, runs in and breaks
the necks of rats that live
under the ripped-up floors.

As for barbed-wire, there's enough
to contain us all as the wind
turns our orders into screams.

ON DUTY AT THE GREAT WALL

Dawn the bruised color of cold iron.
Red dust gathers on the horizon
but comes to nothing.

Sergeants curse. We hug ourselves and spit
into the fire. Emptiness settles around
for a long siege.

And letters from home, meant to console, never
arrive, the distance too much for merely
human feeling.

THE BUS STOPS HERE

When I think of sadness, I think of a young girl
in the back seat of a bus, staring out
of a thick dusty window.

Sadness is mostly quiet, mostly plain
like what she now sees through solitudes
as palpable as glass.

When was the last time you cried? Here
there is no reason for tears, no reason
for much gladness either.

COURTSHIP

I arrive then at the wrong door:
"Come in anyway," she says.
A meal for two is set in crystal.

"Eat," she says, "since you're here." So I sit
and swallow another man's food, drink
of his hope, so much to forgive.

"Stay, if you wish," she says, sorrow,
like smoke, blurring her smile, forgiveness,
like tears, already filling her eyes.

THE DARK LADY UPSTAIRS

In the elevator, descending, the dark lady
and I stare straight ahead,
shy as newlyweds.

She paces far into the night
to where I lose her in a dream
of sandalwood and silk.

When she returns, she will open her door
to admit the only one
she trusts with her mystery.

CASTINGS

I am not here, you are not here.
Two young strangers speak our lines
as if they always had.

Our agent strokes his orange cat
and shrugs. Maybe we could play ghosts...
but no, ghosts don't sweat.

There is no other life but life.
We improvise, walk through walls
that no one knew were there.

THE PLAGUE

The sullen man who lives in the flat below
has three cats, a canister
of oxygen, and groans all night.

Once a week, a woman visits him.
They shout a while. A door slams shut,
followed by tremendous silence.

Loneliness is catching. You feel for the car keys
in your purse, glance down at your wrist
and are gone long before you leave.

THE BRIDGE

The bridge flows easily over
the black water in two directions at once.
I am a man, not a bridge.

I want to be west, deep in the source
of the dark music of consummation,
rapt by the slow movement of lovers.

I want to be east where sunrise, high
in the peaks, promises yet another world.
I am a man, not a bridge.

BELOW

On the western edge of the world, a ship flares
in the sunset. Odysseus lifts his binoculars
and finds a woman on the shore.

So many good-byes, so much desire for distance,
for solitude, those other names for the sea
or for what lies beyond the sea.

Shrugging, he lowers his binoculars
and turns his back to issue a last order,
then goes below to dream again.

RECESSIONAL

He who traveled the world to find
pure distance found only
the next range always receding.

One destination, many names—
Patagonia, Archangel
where tears freeze before they fall.

Even the next room appeared
remote, the woman in it, humming,
hard to reach as the nearest star.

III
NEVERTHELESS

The fall of a child...
The levitation of a poet.
—Aleksander Wat

THE TRAVELER

He who wrote this sat where I sit—
at the window, staring at an illusion
of forest.

The last word he wrote was "hope,"
and here's where his ballpoint ran out of ink.
Or hope.

A slender path runs north through the trees
like a single purpose. I think it might
be his.

PORTRAIT OF THE ARTIST AS A YOUNG MUDLARK

Playing in the ashes, a boy
playing, finds a bone hollowed
by fire. Bitter the taste.

He spits and spits, and finally
blows a sweet cry through the bone—
not his, but also his.

Birds help and the wind and a girl
invisibly singing in the reeds,
and time that his heart beats out.

OFFERINGS

Moss and scarlet leaves on the ancient altar
of the lonely mountain shrine.
What do you think, old man?

They asked you to write a poem in their book,
but does the world really need
another poem?

Now it begins to rain. Not tears. Rain.
And the hand, a little shaky, scrawls,
not tears. Rain.

THE SEEKER

All this time, he sought. And sometimes
found but always the wrong or other thing,
which still, shrugging, he cherished—

bent nail from the True Cross,
charred brick from Troy, wing feather
from a last curlew.

Finally he reached the girl in the tower,
but ancient now, he found precious only
her tears, hard as diamonds.

THIS BODY, THIS WORD

Words come to us slowly, naked,
begging for understanding. We peer
into our little flame and grunt.

Or avert our eyes from the wild procession
of shadows on the walls of the cave.
We haven't learned to dream as yet.

Words full of trouble come, hard
to pronounce, harder to swallow, hardest
of all to keep their secret from silence.

PERFECTION

Perfection—can't get into it the dented
copper pot or the nubile Bosc pear,
or the other muddy yellow boot.

Can't get into it the naked girl
kneeling by the tub, testing the water
with an opalescent palm.

What can be gotten into it fades or spoils
after a few fatal hours under the sun,
itself far from perfect.

MEDITATION ON DISTANCE

This morning's sky holds out no comfort,
no place to hide, a remote,
smoky Jewish sky.

November already half over,
armadas of charred leaves
course through the choked gutters.

A painter of middle distance bends
to his work, which is to bring things
if not home, a little closer.

CANTICLE FOR WINTER

Hope after the death of hope,
mirage of a road at the end of the road,
followed anyway.

Love after the death of love,
a window onto snow, no one to see,
still beautiful.

A bird singing out of season,
consolation after the death
of consolation.

SELF PORTRAIT

Too old for revelation, he made his home
on a small island off the coast
of Maine—nothing fancy:

Ocean pounding the face of rock, wind
flogging the sparse grass, air
charged with outstretched wings.

These he painted as a man would paint
things as they were were he not there
to paint them as they are.

MAKING A LOVE POEM

Let "A" stand for the belovéd, "B"
for a summer's day. Shall we compare them? No,
"A" is more lovely and more temperate—

In short, incomparable, so "B" must do,
"B" a ripe if transient girl—come
with the sun and gone with it in clouds.

Ill-used, she'll wander off, whistling softly
into October, losing leaves, leaving
"A" as yet untouched by human words.

DAUGHTERS OF MUSIC

Daughters of music, brought low these days,
sing on though the wheel is broken,
the almond tree blighted in blighted fields.

We scarcely catch their drift, sisters of wind,
voices of smoke lamenting the broken pitcher
left at the dry well.

Too late now to comfort us, they carol
into the night, lovely, meaningless songs,
obsolete as candles.

WOMAN RUNNING THROUGH RAIN

This is the poem he always wanted to write:
"Woman running through rain," a plain woman
made beautiful by running through rain.

He merely wants to save her, but she is searching
for someone beyond him. She's late, perhaps too late
in her thin summer dress and light coat.

He begins again: "Woman running through rain,"
but can't go on. It may never end, this grief,
never, this beauty running through rain.

TEARS OF THE OLD MAGICIAN

All his tricks desert the old magician—
doves fly out of his hat (if he could find it),
and like a child he claps for more.

See how the pretty girl, made to vanish,
steps forth unharmed, and how, sawed in two,
she is made whole again. And again.

And how tears, seen in a toilet mirror, become
pure unremembering crystal, wanting
for nothing, merely beautiful.

RETURN OF THE ALCHEMIST

We last glimpsed him leaving the park at dusk,
his black greatcoat flapping behind.
Herr Doktor, you forgot your book! But he was gone.

Strange book of alchemical signs
kept in our attic where the children swear
they saw a ghost. Twice! What could it want?

Of course, it had the wrong knowledge. Still,
I've seen its face, pitted and scorched, then woke
at dawn, one meaning away from truth.

THE LAST MIRACLE

Not meaning to be a pilgrim,
not meaning to be redeemed
or entered in the great Book of the Saved.

Not meaning to be a tourist,
meaning nothing, nevertheless,
he found himself on the worn steps.

None of the above, he climbed
up into a cold gray space
not meant to be filled, but filled.

QUARTET

The cello never made it, lost
to us by chance or choice somewhere
between here and there.

We, meanwhile, waited, fiddled
with our instruments, then finally nodded
and began to play without him.

What a strange music—three parts sounded,
one silent, heard only
in the absence of another.

GOUACHE

Sketch of a heavy man in soft grays
and black seated against the faded backdrop
of an old city, Krakow perhaps.

He's not waiting for color to give him life,
or for the glass of darkness on the table
to redden as the artist might have hoped.

He leans to pluck an improvised guitar.
The woman sitting beside him opens her mouth
as if to sing, as if to sing the silence.

MATINEE PERFORMANCE

Spring, and Bach does a little jig in the kitchen.
Stop it, his wife says, as he draws her, laughing,
into the dance, her hands snowy with flour.

It could have happened this way. Smell the strudel—
which, now that you mention it, is burning.
What can she do? Genius nibbles her ear.

Outside, an oriole sings that all is well
for now. Liar! And God Himself—why not?—
snores gently in the next room.

AFFAIRS

Old now, looking at his old wife,
(her eyes bent to the fine work on her lap)
he falls in love again.

But this time quietly, as snow falling
on snow, and so simply you could mistake it
for mere gratitude.

Remember the pretty girl in the almond orchard,
once his love, but where is she? Besides,
he loves this other now.

SWAN SONG

A swan, as it bends to drink, sees itself
upside down in the water, another self
moving where it moves.

Somewhere ahead they may yet converge,
the thing and its reflection become as one,
but not in our time.

Flying now, it seems beautiful
enough for the likes of us, without reflection,
without much thought of the future.